A

BLEEDING

HEART

A BLEEDING HEART is a poetry book.

Written by Thapelo Mafela, Phumudzo Mudau,
Takalani Phathutshedzo

Published by Change Publication

Copyright. © Phumudzo Mudau

All rights reserved. No part of this book may be
reprinted, reproduced stored in a retrieval system, or
transmitted in any form or by any means-
electronically, mechanical, including; photocopying,
recording or in any information storage or retrieval
system, without permission in writing from publishers.

First Edition: 2020. ISBN.

Printed & bound by: Amazon LTT, services.

Book design & layout: Change Publication.

Cover design: Change Publication.

Tel:0735197861/0720700615

Email: Dauphumudzo@gmail.com.

Acknowledgements

With Infinite thanks:

- To Mafela Thapelo for summing up this title and came to collaboration on it.

- To Takalani Phathutshedzo. With your assistance in writing and submission of your poems.

- To the editor and publisher: Change Publication.

- To you, poetry lover you are appreciated.

GODFREY THAPELO MAFELA a
believer of true love who comes from a
small town in Limpopo, far north of
South Africa called MUSINA. An
aspiring Civil engineer and a part time
spoken word poetry writer. He is a
third born of the late Ms
Tshumbedzo Makushu and Mr
Makonde G Mafela . In the 21-century
true love is being replaced with
materialistic love. Nevertheless, my
heart longs to be counted as part of a
few true lovers.

Thapelo Mafela fell in love with poetry at
the age of 16 and he started writing
poetry in the year 2018 yet none of his
poems were ever published,
MR Mafela at the time he only shared
his work with his church mates,
friends and family. In the late 2019 he
was advised to consider sharing his
work with the rest of the world. It was

in 2019 where he started writing spoken words poetry. In 2020 he then decided to publish his work for the first time, due to personal life experience with matters of the heart, he found it benefitting to title this anthology "THE BLEEDING HEART" from the unforgotten, yet forgiven past I have learned. I LEARNED that true love is unconditional, it is an unbreakable and unparalleled fondness and devotion for your partner highly defined by an emotional connection with your partner.

Love as a noun, is not an emotion, but it is an attraction and affection towards a partner or something.

Love as a verb it is something we do, the act of expressing your love(noun) to your partner. It is not selfish nor self-centred.

1. The Bleeding heart

hello!!
yes, my name is true love
I remember it as if it was yesterday,
 my beholder knocking at your door step
you didn't answer
he poured me up unto you
but you couldn't receive me.

was it because my beholder didn't cover himself?
 with cash wear, leather nor cotton cloth
 but with the cheapest fabric ever?
or because I wasn't delivered with a Ferrari, poche,
or polo, yet I was delivered by a pedestrian.
is it because the delivery man wasn't good looking
to your eyes?

it is unfortunate that you looked for me with ALL
YOUR HEART
yet you only looked for me in the wrong places,
my beholder couldn't keep me long enough for you
to come around
only god knows when.
he gave me to another.

2.   Only if he knew

He saw her for the first time and he felt like his heart skipped a beat.

Pure beauty! An ANGEL without wings,

She was lovely in all ways you can imagine..."PHYSICALY"!'

He pored his heart to and she gladly received it, she filled her cup

In his heart he wrote "she is mine to marry" .... only if he knew!

His intensions where not pure

Only if he knew. She is a heart collector

Only if he knew

her bag is filled with other boys' hearts

which she collected from different towns.

Only if he knew that his number was saved as "RENT MONEY"

Only if he knew that within few months

his ear will be crashed in tinny pieces.

It is Only safe to say that He would have kept his love

he would have saved his heart for another.

3. The ideal man

Women are very artistic,

when it comes to painting a picture of their ideal man

They go all the way

One would say "tall, dark and handsome, loving and caring ..."

And the other could say "short, funny, badly, companionate etc."

We all want good things

Many times, the package comes incomplete or mismatched,

for example; The "HUNK" without the brains and a loving heart

A TRUE LOVER without the looks or money

It is said that, "love is a matter between two hearts"

so why do we always drag our Brains into the matter?

Let not your Brains meddle with matters of your heart.

Love drinks from a well of beauty,

And beauty is in the eyes of the beholder.

Love joints two hearts into one

the more you give it, the more you have it

Love them with their incomplete complexities.

4. What is wrong with me?

what is wrong with me?

funny enough I can`t find anything

I thought I could be a great runner and chased
   you

I chased you as I was running away from her

 not knowing that you are also chasing someone,

 I thought you were jogging.

she loves me,

I love you, you love him

and possibly she loves another.

at the end we all love another.

the irony!

are we the unfortunate?

we long for it yet we don't grab it when it
    comes our way

Will we ever receive it?

Do we even know it?

5. Lesson learned

I never thought this day would ever come

I always thought you and I will never be things of
the past

I am afraid it came to pass,

you and I are history, a thing of the past,

just yesterday you said I was forever yours

and today you are telling me the opposite.

It is well, it is well with my heart

its a good thing that I cry in my closet

I can`t lie and say I don't think of you

missing you has become a nom unto me

by 'YOU' I meant OUR good memories

as for 'U' I mean you, U taught me the lessons of life

and I learned the hard way

Now I know that ''I LOVE YOU TOO'' is based on conditions

Now I KNOW that there is a silver lining between ''I DO and I DON`T ''

6. Nothing more to say

There is nothing more   I can do

 There is nothing more to say

I gave all my heart unto thee,

 As big as it was you took it.

You convinced me that you would take good care
of it

You said regardless of how complex it could ever
be you will diligently care for it

Your sweat words made me believe it, I was a full!

A full who listened to his mined and not to his
heart

Now look at me! I have been collecting pieces of
my heart for as long as I can remember

Not only did you break it but you broke it to
countless pieces.

Unto my porter I am forever grateful

 I couldn`t do it on my own

He always finds a way to mend my heart

Is there any other porter like him?

I now have a beautiful, eunuch loving heart

There is nothing more that I can do Apart from
moving on with my life

There is northing more to say Apart from saying"
good by love"

It is said that "Life is for the living" **so live life love
life.**

Do you and I will do me!

7. If you fall in love with me

This is not some regular poem

I am simply making things clear for you

So that If you happen you fall in love with me

 you know what you are getting into

I am an all or nothing person

I go out of my way for love

If I happen to fall in love with you

 I won`t be limited to loving you

First thing I think of when I wake up

and the last thing I think of before I sleep would be
you

I will be head over heals for your smile, your
giggle…. the funny gesture you give me,

The look in your eyes

The time spent with you saying nothing

and then feel like we said a lot to each other.

If you happen to fall in love with me

 Expect someone with his own view points

Have a room for my mistakes because I make a lot
of them

The good thing is, I always learn from my mistakes.

Never play with my feeling because you may win
the game

 but surely lose a jam of a man for a life time

Don`t just fall in love with me, fall in love with my
infinite complexities.

8. Lies

Trapped in the web of love?

You are not alone

I just can`t stop to wonder "**Why**"

Why is the heart so full of deceit?

When I think of

 Its "heart" saddens

It hurts me deeply when I see her jumping over the moon

After hearing another man saying "I love you" to her

The thing is, I know that he doesn't I mean it

 he is too old to be her father.

Could it be that she is not used to these words?

9. Her Beauty

the picture was vivid enough for me to see at a distance

but the circumstances wouldn't let me

and I convinced myself that it was only a marriage.

she had it all, my god! the young lady was beautiful in all angles my eyes could use.

with just a glance at her, I was convinced that the word beautiful was invented after her

 I pictured her on the worst outfit ever yet it looked dope on her

10. Too good to be true

I dived too deep

 Because I was convinced

That I am a good swimmer.

Now I am not sure if I can swim at all,

I AM DROWNING!

I am so deep in love

 And I can't breathe properly

Your insecurities are pulling me up every time I try
to swim in it.

what went wrong?

 when we started, it was all great

 just as we pictured our ideal love story

what happened to the trust you had in me?

perhaps the session has changed

I now see a shadow everywhere I go

 they all said, "it was too good to be

11. A letter to my unborn daughter

'I LOVE YOU'

The most used words by boys,

Meaning almost nothing to them

yet a great deal to girls.

Do not be deceived by how cynical they look when saying it

It's a camelish.

I am telling you this before you are born

 so that you can now that daddy loves you.

'I LOVE YOU'

These are the words I will tell you every morning

So that they don't sound unfamiliar when they say them unto you.

I once loved and not once heartbroken. I
   am not an angel but I did break few
   hearts and it wasn't my fault I guess in
   the process of loving we win some and
   lose some. You get heartbroken and
   find someone to mend your heart. My
   heart has experienced bleeding for
   several times. First in high school.
   Second in university. Last after
   graduating. One can't really lose to
   count heartfelt moments. I had many
   reasons while writing such touching
   poems. I guess after going through
   what's below you are to feel me more,
   but it's life we all go through staff.
   Mine might be worse or better than
   yours. But a heart break is a heart break
   with a small knife or big one we all feel
   pain.

Life became a series of sordid roller
coaster rides, spinning now and tossing
me then; it seemed I became lost in my
own dilemma; and I stopped loving. I
have been lonely for the most part of
my life. I had lost touch with the world
of passion, affection and emotion. I do
not want to cry for what brews in my
heart and soul for her but I am crying
for what I have missed all along.

Is it wrong for me to fall in love? Is it
wrong that I should chase after my
desire? Is it wrong that I should be
sincere about emotions and passion
that seem to flow endlessly like a river
from the bosom of mother earth, its
beginning is never known and its end
just flooding the rivers and oceans? Is it
wrong that I should want to live my life
like any other normal human being?

Well, I have lost loved ones before; whom
I cherished so dearly, but they never
knew how much so and those who did,
took mg love for them for granted.
What if I do not make it that further in
life? Would the one I loved so dearly
know how intense the storm that

brewed in my being was? So I made a promise to myself, to say each day how much she means to me and "to avoid that circumstance where there is no second chance to tell her how I feel" because if the sun never rises on my soul again, her knowledge of her throne in my heart would suffice for a seeming unrequited love one that has shaken the earth and blown the wind and burned the fire.

I remember this breakup that made me to say to myself "I never will show this kindness to an ordinary woman I do fall in love with again. Ever; all that is at your disposal is just a tip of the ice berg, and that is because of love. It is the drive in one's soul that makes them do things that seem somewhat overboard, but then again, can I be blamed? I thought I have loved before...I must say that, then, I reckon, it was child's play, for the love that comes in the forties is more intense than a hurricane in a tea cup.

Life can be unfair and bleak; love is warm and cuddly; but where forth may one seek consolation? Whence it cometh, doth it justice proper or not? Just thinking out loud, lest you think I am hallucinating.

But then I felt a need of love and in me it was a call like: I want to live again; I want to smile again; I want to run after a woman and fall on the green together; I want to picnic with and feed a woman with my hands; I just want to love the girl of my dream. To some people she may not seem lovable or endearing but to me she is better than.

I just wanted that singular opportunity to show the sparkle in my affections towards her.

I am just another man in love - a special man in love with a special woman...

1. THE WAY WE ARE

There is a way that people think

No matter what our particular backgrounds are

There is one thing we all have in common

Who are you?

Who are your people?

How did you come to be you?

We all make difficult choices

Decisions haven't always been good

Everyone wrestles with "the way we are"

 Humans! We have always made choices

At a point of mistakes or laws of life

Take heart! It is the way we are.

2.   LIVING ON THE RUN

People ruin their lives

They then blame the Lord for it

Biblically that's in Proverbs 19:3

It is easier to do what you want

In whatever you want

With whatever you want

But is living on the run?

That you want.

With unlimited wants to be on top

To some; it has been difficult situation

The haste to make it

The competition to make it

Pressed to make it

Or the hunger strike.

3. IS IT DIFFICULT TIMES YOU WANT?

What do you want?

There come difficulty times in your life

Facing your most difficult night

As you think about a stressed-out "YOU"

Consider the tough choices you have to make

The things you don't want

What do you want?

It is a simple question

Important than your own life

What kind of decision will you make?

Wanting to do good things?

But have such a hard time doing them

You don't have to be tired

Just do what you want.

4. THE STRUGGLE IN DOING GOOD

Sometimes outside pressures

Sometimes surrounding environment

Can play a role in our bad decisions

We might know the right thing to do

But fears cause us to make wrong choices

Haste, hurry, fast line, and easy way

Sometimes cause us to make wrong choices

It becomes hard to do good

Refuse to listen "outside pressures"

If you are led away to serve good

Don't be destroyed by the struggle of doing
    good

If your good is low than others

Keep it low; so, your good

For a long time;

Doing good has been a struggle to most.

5.   HIS WILL FOR YOUR LIFE

You might ask

What is God's will for your life?

What choice should you make?

About going to school or university.

What about your job?

What about your relationships?

Which one is God's choice for you?

The will of God is for everyone

To choose life not death

You are part of His will.

6.   WE'RE AFRAID IT'S SERIOUS

Perhaps not as common as it used to be

I seem to have struck a chord

Off key I may sound

I am afraid life took a serious turn

It is no longer how I do things

It is about how I used to do things

Life in its form; we are afraid.

Aging is an issue; it's serious.

The responsibilities that comes with it

It is no longer I living for me

But I living for family

It has become the way to live

The streets are no longer safe

Freedom at an expense of one's life

Everyone in war; not physically

But emotionally

We are afraid; it's serious.

7. THE ONLY PAIN

The only pain known to me

Is to love and never loved

To love someone who'll never love you

My heart bleeped painfully

She had each and every quality

The desires of my heart

Living each day with wishes

Smiling with fake hope

Someone has a similar situation

Though I would not wish

I have learned what it feels too much

You may be educated and self sufficient

But that has nothing to do with loving

This pain was unpreventable

The only pain known to me.

8.   A BLEEDING HEART

What do I get in return?

A bleeding heart

I gave you my heart

You returned it bleeding

I gave you my trust

You returned trusting issues

I gave you my securities

You returned insecurities

I had hope in you

You returned me hopeless

I pulled my bleeding heart

So, I no longer love you

I blocked my memory

So, I no longer think of you

I cleansed my eyes

So, I no longer see you

My heart is speaking

"All on its own"

As we know that the more, we grow; we all
   need love, we all need someone, but
   not just someone. A person who will
   make us complete, someone who will
   make us feel love and loved. Who will
   make us look deep in ourselves and
   believe in ourselves? You can't enjoy
   what you love to do without the person
   you love. Sometimes you have to open
   up your heart to the world and let your
   HEART choose whom it loves.
   together I was so much in love even if I
   have to use my last breath, I would use
   it loving her. However, Things started
   to change we fight; we argue.

I don't know where it went wrong, she
   cheats on me again and again I kept on
   taking her back because I didn't know
   that she doesn't love me. I was just a
   rebound.

I give up on love I don't want to fall in
love anymore. I want nothing to do
with love my heart is still bleeding I
want nothing to with girls. All that we
built, the love that was meant to keep
she lost it; I lose it. I was just a boy not
knowing matters of a heart.

1.   Help me lord

Dear lord I bow down before you as I

Kneel down before your throne lord.

I came to you lord with a heart broken

When thoughts are unprofitable

 I came to You as you are the source of
    everything.

Help me lord

Give me the strength because the strength I

Have is washing away

Help me to trust you more

I Trust you with the plans you have with my
    future

In your word you say" I God I will

Command blessing and the blessing will chase

Me and overtake me"

Help me lord to hold

On my vision and trust the process

Lord am all my knees when I know

that when I pray you hear me

And

you will answer my prayers lord I know

all things work together to those Who

love god

You are all I need lord, all I want

help me lord.

2. Not anymore

Am not taking it anymore

 You pushed me over the edge

You always make me look bad

AND Look guilty

YOU always make me apologizing

Keep cleaning up after you messed up

All I Want was somebody to love

Somebody holds

Somebody I can be happy to be with

but not any more

I know that I told you "I can't leave without
    and

imagine myself loving some else"

 yes! its true but not anymore

I can leave without you

better to be with someone I can be happy with

Than to with be unhappy with someone

Am leaving you I don't want you not anymore

I don't need your sympathy

I don't want to hear your meaningless
         charming words

3.   Red Rose

Where do I begin?

 How do I describe "beauty"?

Your adequate beauty

even the pen on my hand can't

 I want to breath down on your neck and

Whisper slowly sweet songs

 I want to smell you like am taking last breathe

Grab you by your wrist and pull you back

4. Do I?

I know that my heart is broken and am angry

I don't even know what am thinking

Am still hurt, obsessed with feelings

Wanting to end everything!

Hatreds and thought are unprofitable. Do I?

Do I have to think about it?

Thought are of suicidal

Broken thought and soul wanting to let GO

Do I have to?

 I mean is that even a solution?

5.   HOME ALONE

Siting home alone in my room facing four

walls wondering Where are they. How am

I going to find my way.

Pondered deep about the past

Thinking about the things that are not created
    by man

This home alone was supposed to be my home

Time alone, My me time. Lot of voice in my
    head

Telling me not to stop

Not to give up

6. you did it again

How can you?

How can you do that to me?

Oh lord why don't I see this one coming

How did we get here?

I said do you remember…

The day I said am sorry

It's like you were not hearing me

Why? You did it again, how can you?

You always said this is the last time, but you
    did it

Again, you were lying to me, you never meant
    what you said.

www.ingramcontent.com/pod-product-compliance
Lightning Source LLC
Chambersburg PA
CBHW071257130726
47998CB00003B/1223